Soap Making Explained

Soap Making for Beginners

The Art of Soap Making, Supplies, Ingredients, Types of Soaps, Basic Soap Making Techniques, Packaging and More!

By Cynthia Cherry

Copyrights and Trademarks

Disclaimer and Legal Notice

Foreword

Soap is an ionic compound that came from a combination of base and acid. Its primary purpose back then is to clean materials before it became a household item for personal hygiene. Today, most hygienic soaps particularly bath soaps are made from fatty acids like vegetable oils and animal fats that's combined with alkaline solution like potash and lye. It undergoes a chemical change known as saponification.

The art of soap making has been around for hundreds of years and it has quite a history. As you may have guessed, the methods that people used back then is very different from today's modern techniques. There never was a standard way of creating soaps. It's not made with the same material either, and similar to creating candles various supplies, ingredients, temperatures and curing factors come into play. If you really want to master this old art, the first thing you need to do is decide which soap making technique is best for you because as you will find out later in this book – there are LOTS of it.

There are various techniques of making your own soap, and once you learn the basics of how to make one, you can easily get started. According to soap experts, the main reason why it's satisfying to create your own soap is because it has 'character,' which is something that most commercial soaps in the market lack. So, if this is your first time, you're in for an artistic treat! If you've already tried one, then you already know how amazing it is and perhaps you would want to learn more!

Making a DIY (do – it – yourself) soap from the comfort of your home is not just easy and inexpensive but also a creative and fulfilling experience. For some people, it's quite satisfying when they can create their own unique bar of soap and use it for bathing and showering.

Whether you're someone who is passionate about arts and crafts, or you're looking for a natural alternative to various commercial soaps out there, creating your own soap is both fun and engaging. You can even get your family involved in the process and add your own 'flavor' of soap. You can also turn it into a home – based business or a holiday giveaway! Whatever your purpose is, this book will cover all the basic and advance techniques you need from the soap –

making process to packaging, we've got you covered. Get ready for one bubbly adventure!

Table of Contents

Introduction to the Art of Soap Making

There are 2 types of hygienic soaps. The first one is made out of lye or sodium hydroxide which is solid, and the second one is made out of potash or potassium hydroxide which is usually soft and liquid. Soaps made out of potash are the commonly used soap making ingredient back in the day because people can extract alkali material from wood ashes before cooking it oven an open fire along with animal fat. Old – fashioned soap - makers and pioneers store the homemade soaps in ceramic rocks and boxes and use it when necessary. Historically speaking though, lye also refers to potash but true lye (made out of sodium hydroxide) is already a modern chemical that's now commonly used in making soaps particularly the commercial products because it needs an industrial setting since it's quite dangerous due to high alkaline content. In fact, lye is often used in murder dramas and crime shows due to its ability to digest human and animal tissues. A single drop of lye can easily burn the skin and even cause eye damage if it's not immediately washed away. Due to the potential danger of the ingredients, it's very important that you learn the materials used in soap – making before you try it out. This book will guide you on how you can properly and safely create soap.

Basic Soap – Making Techniques

Before we get into the details of the different methods of soap – making, it's also essential to know what soap is from a chemical perspective. According to crafts experts, soap is the product of a basic chemical reaction produced by lye and fats/ oils. If you carefully choose the right combination of ingredients such as fragrance, colorant, essential oils, and other products, you can create a charming product that has its own 'flavor' or 'character' that even commercial soaps cannot compete with.

Here are the four basic methods of soap – making:

- **Melt and Pour:** This is the easiest technique of making soap because all you have to do is to pretty much melt the pre – made blocks of soap in order to add your own set of ingredients/ fragrance.

- **Cold – Process:** This is the most common technique of soap – making from scratch using lye and oils.

- **Hot Process:** This is simply a variation of the cold – process technique where soaps are cooked using an oven or a crockpot.

- **Re - batching:** This is a method where bars of soap are being grinded and re – blended with water, milk or other ingredients.

Pros and Cons of Soap – Making Methods

Each soap – making technique has its own variations as well as pros and cons. Through reviewing the two most commonly used methods which are melt and pour, and cold – process can help you choose which process best suit a beginner like you. This section will give you an overview of the two major techniques used in making soaps.

Method #1: Melt and Pour Soap - Making

Making a soap using this method is similar to creating a cake with a cake mix already. All you have to pretty much do is to "bake" it. This is why it's a perfect method for beginners like you since you won't really need to mind the basic soap ingredients and customization of the recipe – you simply just melt and pour because the hard part has already been done for you. It's easy, convenient, and safe to do.

If you use the melt & pour technique, you just need to buy pre – made blocks of soap that are usually uncolored and unscented. You can get soap base from a supplier or craft store near you. The process involves melting the soap base using a double boiler or your microwave. Once the soap is thoroughly melted, you can then add your handpicked charms like colors, scents, and other additives you like.

Once you're done with that, you can put the melted soap in a mold and wait for it to harden for a period of time. Viola! You're done! Easy right? We'll discuss more about this method in the upcoming chapters. For now check out the materials you'll need as well as the pros and cons of this technique so that you'll have an idea:

Materials:

- Tabletop or any clean workspace
- Double boiler or microwave
- Heat bowl for the microwave
- Whisks and spoons
- Pre – made block/s of soap base
- Measuring spoons
- Scented fragrance, soap colorant or other additives you like
- Soap molder

Pros and Cons of Melt & Pour Soap

Consider the following:

Pros:

- Easy to do and a very cheap way to create your own soap
- You don't have to mix the lye chemical which can be dangerous
- You just need basic ingredients to complete the process
- You don't need a lot of materials
- It's a ready – made soap that you can use as soon as it hardens

Cons:

- You have no control over the ingredients used in the pre – made block soap base
- This method is not as natural compared to other techniques since most soap base manufacturers already added chemicals to make the soap much lather or to better allow it to melt

- Your end product is only as good as the soap base you will buy

Method #2: Cold Process Soap - Making

If the first method is similar to using a cake mix and just baking it, the cold – process technique is basically creating a cake or in this case, a soap from scratch. This method is for crafty people who already had some experience in creating a basic soap or those who wanted to have control over the ingredients used in the soap base. The advantage is that it's up to you on what goes into the pot and you can also make the content as natural as you desire. However, the set-up and process is quite complicated compared to the melt and pour method, and you may need to learn basic techniques of soap – making before you try doing this (which we will cover in this book).

In a nutshell, the cold – process soap making involves working with raw materials. You will need to heat the oils that you want to use in your soap up and boil it up to 100 degrees before adding the lye – water mixture so that it will blend in your sap until it thickens. Once the mixture reaches trace, this is the only time you can start adding colorant, fragrance and whatever additives you like. You need to pour it into the mold and wait for 24 hours before it hardens. After which, you need to wait another 4 weeks to cure before you can actually use it. It's quite a long and tedious process but for a crafty person, this is a more personalized technique.

We'll discuss more about the cold - process method in the upcoming chapters. For now check out the materials you'll need as well as the pros and cons of this technique so that you'll have an idea:

Materials:

- Tabletop and clean workspace with access to a heat source and water
- Vegetable oils or animal fats
- 1 pitcher of lye – water solution
- Tools and Equipment including a soap pot
- Colorant (natural/ synthetic), essential oils, additives and fragrance
- Soap mold

- A cool and dry place for the curing period

Pros and Cons of Cold - Process Soap

Consider the following:

Pros:

- Your end product is made from raw materials and ingredients that you desire
- You can control what goes in the pot
- You can customize/ personalize your own recipe into unlimited variations

Cons

- You need to have ingredients and tools to begin
- You need to know how to safely use the lye solution because it can be a dangerous substance
- It take longer to create and more cleanup is needed
- You need to wait a for days and weeks before you can use the soap

The method you will choose doesn't really determine how successful your end product will be, it all boils down to how patient you are, and how you can follow instructions. Once you already learn the basic, you can start exploring other advance techniques and be more creative in the soaps you're going to make.

The next chapter will give you the basic ingredients of soap making such as the fragrance, essential oils, herbs, and colorants you can use.

Chapter One: Basic Ingredients Used in Soap Making

As mentioned in the previous chapter, most soap – makers especially beginners use the melt and pour method as it is much easier to create rather than making one from raw materials. You can easily buy a ready – made soap base from a soap supplier or a craft store near you. You will simply melt the soap base into liquid form before adding in other soap ingredients like fragrance, oils, herbs, and colorants then pouring it into soap molds. The main benefit of using a ready – made soap base is that you don't need to mind about the chemical reaction procedure to create the end product, making it easier and more convenient for crafters to elegantly add their personal touch and uniquely color or shape their soaps.

Various artistic presentations of handcrafter bars are usually made using the melt and pour method. There are also different types of ready – made soap bases in the market; you can choose to buy a "true soap" or soap base made out of synthetic detergents.

In this chapter, we'll focus on the basic building blocks you need to create a bar of soap. You'll learn the basic materials that you need to use if you're going to apply the basic melt and pour method.

Basic Melt & Pour Method

Prepare the following materials:

- The first thing you need is a great **melt and pour soap base** which you can buy from your local craft store or soap supplier. You can also order it online.

- Next is a **chopping utensil**. It's up to you if you want to use a knife but if it's you're first time to do this, we highly recommend that use a chopping utensil as it is usually easier to handle and control. If you're going to work with your kids, make sure to supervise them, or better yet do the cutting yourself to avoid any mishaps. A chopping utensil can cost around $4. It's best to use a scraper cutter which you can buy from any cooking store or kitchenware section in groceries.

- You also need a **heat safe container**. This material is very important because this is where you're going to heat your soap base. It's also microwaveable and can be used in double boiler as well if that's what you prefer.

- You need to purchase **quality soap molds**. You can also use Tupperware or yogurt container but it is best if you use soap molds because it can give your end product that extra professional look.

- You also need to prepare **droppers, spoon, and rubbing alcohol** as well as **fragrance oils and essential oils** of your choice – you can easily buy these from craft store as well.

Fragrance Oils vs. Essential Oils

Fragrance oils are usually made out of synthetic aroma chemicals and not natural products. Don't worry though because most fragrance oils are tested for carcinogenity, skin irritants, allergens, and safety by the Research Institute for Fragrance Materials. The reason why most soap - makers love using fragrance oils is because it is available in various flavors; fragrance oils come in chocolate, strawberry, root beer, raspberry and all other artificial flavors that you can't get from natural oils.

On the other hand, essential oils are made out of natural products. It often comes from the zest of an orange or lemon, and even from the buds of a flower. However, the flavors are only limited to what is available in nature. It doesn't also mean that if you can find it in nature, it can be used as an essential oil. For instance, even if you use lilac flowers which smell great, you can't turn it into an essential oil. There are many flowers and fruits that don't contain enough aroma compounds which can be extracted by manufacturers which is why soap – makers turn to artificial fragrance oils.

Choosing between the two oils depend on your preference. So, it's up to you if you want to stick using essential oils but keep in mind that you're limited in your choices. You can also opt to use fragrance oils which are fruity and also fun to use. However, you should know that fragrance oils sometimes discolor in the soap. Using essential oils can also turn your soap mold into yellow or green in color due to the natural dew of the fruit. If that happens, the next soap you're going to make using the same soap mold will have a slight cast of that color.

Let's Get Started!

Here's the materials you'll need if you want to create a soap with fragrance/ essential oils:

- 4 oz. soap base (must be clear)

- 2 ml. of tangerine essential oil (or any flavor of your choice)
- Soap Mold
- Spoon
- Heat safe container
- Dropper
- Spray bottle (filled with rubbing alcohol)

Step by Step Procedure:

Step #1: The first thing you need to do is to use your chopping utensil and chop up your soap base. You should chop it up into cube sizes because it melts in the heat safe container evenly once you pop it into the microwave later.

Step #2: After chopping your soap base into cubes, you can put it all in the heat safe container or your double boiler. It's also best to cover the heat safe container with a plastic wrap so that the soap gets to keep its moisture inside.

Step #3: Next step is to place it in your microwave for about 30 seconds. This is the ideal time that your soap base needs to create a good heat formation without scorching or boiling it. If you happen to boil or scorch it, the soap base will not only smell bad but also turns into a yellowish color. You may still use it but don't expect it to have a great quality.

Step #4: Once the soap base is already thoroughly melted in your double boiler/ microwave, you can now add your essential or fragrance oil.

Step #5: It's up to you if you want to use a dropper for your fragrance or essential oil. We recommend that you only drop around ¼ oz. of essential or fragrance oil per pound of your soap base (4 bars of soap).

Step #6: After adding your essential/ fragrance oil, you then need to stir it using a spoon. It's very important that you stir it well so that it will be thoroughly mixed with the soap base otherwise the oil can float to the surface of the soap that will create an oil slit, or it could leave a mark in your molds.

Step #7: The next step is to pour the soap solution into your soap mold.

Step #8: After pouring the soap solution into the mold, you should spray a bit of rubbing or isopropyl alcohol into the soap for the purpose of breaking up the surface tension of the bubbles. This could give your end product a smooth finished appearance.

Step #9: Now all you need to do is let the soap solution harden for a couple of hours before using it.

Using Herbs and Colorants

In this section, you'll learn how to use herbs and colorants in your melt and pour soap base. You'll also get tips on how to create soap bars that really pop with color. There are a few options for you to choose from when using colorants for soaps. Check out the following:

Oxides

All natural color is what oxides is all about. These are the materials used to put coloring in cosmetic products such as eye shadows, lipsticks and the likes. Oxides are relatively cheaper and it creates a dull color in your soap. These are stable colorants but they're also oil – based, and your melt and pour is water – based which means if you use these colorants, you need to be extra careful to create a great melt and pour soap bar.

Mica

Another colorant you can use for your soap base is a mica. Mica is a colorant that is mined from the ground and it's a flat platelet. It's quite dull in color but if you shine and cut it similar to a diamond, it's known to refracts and reflects color which is why if you choose to use this colorant, you'll notice that the powder has a shining and shimmering quality to it making it a perfect colorant for eye shadow makeup and soaps! Micas can be coated with food, drug and cosmetic color as well as oxides. It comes from a natural source and the color can also be produce synthetically. So, if you want to use a natural colorant, oxides are your best choice but if you want to make your soap pop or glitter up, you can opt for a mica colorant.

Labcolor

Labcolor can also be coated with food, drug and cosmetic color. They are similar to food colorings because they are not natural unlike micas. Speaking colorants, you can also choose food colors in your soap. Labcolors are your best choice if you want to try various colorants for your soap because it's available in 140 colors – now that's a lot of options!

Just a quick tip though: if you want to avoid creating spots in your end product, make sure to dilute your labcolors in water because they are very concentrated substance.

Here are some tips on how you can dilute labcolors in water:

- Use your heat safe container and pour in about 10 ml. of labcolor with 8 oz. of water.

- Stir it up nicely and you're done!

- Make sure to store it to the fridge if you want it to last for a long period of time. If you don't like to put the labcolor mixture inside the fridge, you can just add a water – based preservative like Optiphen in it.

Labcolors are also water – soluble which means that it can fade or create a color migration around your soap. You will also get it if you use a food coloring, so the trick to ensuring that the color in your soap stay crisp and doesn't fade away is to use a non – bleeding liquid; these are made out of oxide alterine that are already mixed and dissolved into a glycerin so that you can conveniently and easily use it.

Let's Get Started!

Here's the materials you'll need if you want to create a soap using colorants:

- 8 oz. soap base (must be clear)
- 8 oz. white soap base
- 1/10 ounces of ultramarine violet colorant
- ¼ oz. lavender buds
- ¼ oz. lavender fragrance oil
- Heat safe container
- Dropper
- Soap mold

- Spoon

- Spray bottle (filled with rubbing alcohol)

Step by Step Procedure:

Step #1: The first thing you need to do is to use your chopping utensil and chop up your soap base (both the clear one and the white one). You should chop it up into cube sizes because it melts in the heat safe container evenly once you pop it into the microwave later.

Step #2: After chopping your soap base into cubes, you can put it all in the heat safe container or your double boiler. It's also best to cover the heat safe container with a plastic wrap so that the soap gets to keep its moisture inside.

Step #3: Next step is to place it in your microwave for about 30 seconds. This is the ideal time that your soap base needs to create a good heat formation without scorching or boiling it. If you happen to boil or scorch it, the soap base will not only smell bad but also turns into a yellowish color. You may still use it but don't expect it to have a great quality.

Step #4: Once your soap bases are melting, pour in a bit of rubbing alcohol into a small dish container. Take a few scoops of oxide colorant and simply mix it up using a stirrer so that you can pour it later in your melted soap bases.

Step #5: After taking out your soap base from the microwave, you can add in fragrance oil using a dropper. Make sure to pour in around 0.25 oz. or ¼ oz. of fragrance oil per pound of soap bar then mix it up. If you want to produce an intense, vibrant color, make sure to use a clear soap base for the colorant to pop out. For white soap base, you'll pretty much get a pastel shade color.

Step #6: After adding your essential/ fragrance oil and herbs, you then need to stir it using a spoon. It's very important that you stir it well so that it will be thoroughly mixed with the soap base otherwise the fragrance oil can float to the surface of the soap that will create an oil slit, or it could leave a mark in your molds.

Step #7: The next step is to pour the soap solution into your soap mold.

Step #8: After pouring the soap solution into the mold, you should spray a bit of rubbing or isopropyl alcohol into the soap for the purpose of breaking up the surface tension of the bubbles. This could give your end product a smooth finished appearance.

Step #9: Now all you need to do is let the soap solution harden for a couple of hours to a few days before using it. However, keep in mind that if you use herbs like lavender buds, it can die and turn into brown color on your soap after a few weeks. It's only good looking and vibrant a few days right after it hardens.

Chapter Two: Swirled Layers and Embedding with Melt and Pour Soap Base

In this chapter, you're going to learn how to do a swirl soap using the melt and pour method as well as how to embed objects and soap objects into your soap base. The steps you'll learn here are very simple and easy to follow but it requires a bit of patience especially if you want to create nice layers within your soap bar. Keep in mind that the materials you should use must be skin – safe especially if you're planning to make soaps for kids. Make sure that the object you embed later on are also non – hazardous.

Swirling Using Melt and Pour Soap

Here are the tips and tricks that you need to know before we proceed on the step by step procedure.

Tip #1: Make sure to use the same brand of melt and pour base soap if you want to create a swirl soap. If you use different brands of soap base, it will contain different ingredients that can evaporate at different rates which can cause the layers to separate; your end product will be a mess.

Tip #2: It's also best to use non – bleeding colorants because this will prevent the colors to fade away and combine in another swirl layer. Non – bleeding liquid colorants containing oxide ingredients are suspended in glycerin designed for soap – makers that they can easily and conveniently use for melt and pour soap base projects.

Tip #3: When you're making a swirl loaf, it's best that you use a loaf mold and not just any flat silicon baking sheet. This is because you need depth for your melt and pour soap base.

Tip #4: We highly recommend that you use a spoon, fork or even chopstick because these materials will aid you during the swirling phase.

Tip #5: Don't rush. Creating layers of swirls in your soap will take time especially if you're planning in doing various colors and layers in your soap.

Tip #6: It's also best to use contrasting colorants (though it's not required) but it creates an appeal and makes each swirled layer stand out once it hardens.

Let's Get Started!

Here's the materials you'll need if you want to create a swirled kind of soap:

- 2 pounds of soap base (must be clear)
- ½ pound of soap base (white)
- Non – bleeding liquid colorant (pink, blue and purple)
- Gold Mica
- 1 ounce of Yuzu fragrance
- 2 ½ pounds of loaf mold

- Small cups or containers for mixing the colorants

- Spoon

- Dropper

- Heat safe container (large)

- Spray bottle (filled with rubbing alcohol)

Step by Step Procedure:

Step #1: Make sure to melt your (2 pounds) of clear soap base using your heat safe container in the microwave or double boiler. Just like the basic steps in previous exercises. The layers for the soap base are often just 2 ounces at maximum, making it not convenient to re – melt the soap base every single time.

Step #2: Once the clear soap base has already melted, you can now use your dropper to add the Yuzu fragrance or any fragrance you desire.

Step #3: On the very first layer using the loaf mold, you just need to create a very thin layer (around 2 ounces or less of the melted clear soap). Don't forget that every layer is scented so that the soap would smell nice from top to bottom.

Step #4: The next step is to take a pinch of the gold mica and drop it into the first layer of your soap base. You will notice that once you're already cutting your hardened soap base, the gold mica will appear like a fairy dust, adding aesthetic to your finished product.

Step #5: After doing the first layer, you need to wait for it to harden. You can determine if your soap is fully hardened by slightly blowing. If you happen to see that it creates ripples on the surface that only means your soap is not yet fully hardened.

Step #6: While you're waiting, the next thing you can do is to put your non – bleeding colorant (whichever color you want on the first layer) in the small dish with water and stir it up using a spoon.

Step #7: Once the first layer of your soap base finally hardens, you can now spray it with a bit of rubbing alcohol and pour in just a thin layer of colorant over the first layer of your soap base. Keep in mind that you are going to do around 12 layers so make sure you get the first one right.

Step #8: After doing that, you can now pour in the melted white soap base on top of the first layer with colorant as it will provide contrast and make the first layer of colorant stand out. When you're pouring the melted white soap base, you just need to drizzle it and do an "S – pattern." Take your spoon, and just run it through once. Don't mix it up! Spray a bit of rubbing alcohol and wait for it to develop a thin layer of skin on top.

Step #9: After doing that, you can now create succeeding layers by following the same steps but using different colorants or fragrances. Make sure to pour in white melted soap base per layer if you want your colorants to pop out.

Step #10: Repeat the same steps per layer and once you reach the top of the loaf mold, wait for your soap base to harden completely before using it.

Embedding Objects in Melt & Pour Soap

Here are the tips and tricks that you need to know before we proceed on the step by step procedure.

Tip #1: Make sure that the object you're going to embed in your soap is age – appropriate. What this means is that, for instance you're going to create a bar for young children or babies make sure that the object you'll embed in the soap isn't something that they can choke on.

Tip #2: Never use inappropriate objects that can cut or scrape the user.

Tip #3: If you're going to embed a soap within the soap itself, make sure to use non – bleeding colorants to avoid fading or mixing with other colors.

Tip #4: Temperature is very essential. The soap base should be melted between 120 degrees Fahrenheit and 125 degrees Fahrenheit (or depending on the soap base you bought). Make sure to ask your soap supplier about the ideal temperature for pouring embedded objects in their soap base.

Tip #5: Never mix brands of soap bases. If you use different brands of soap base, it will contain different ingredients that can evaporate at different rates which can cause the layers to separate; your end product will be a mess.

Let's Get Started!

Here's the materials you'll need if you want to create an embedded object soap:

- Soap base (must be clear)
- Labcolor (for this exercise, we'll use blue – mix and aqua colorants)
- Fragrance oil
- Object you want to embed (you can buy various objects online or from a craft store)
- Iridescent glitter
- Small cups or containers for mixing the colorants
- Soap mold
- Spoon
- Dropper

- Heat safe container

- Spray bottle (filled with rubbing alcohol)

Step by Step Procedure:

Step #1: The first thing you need to do is to use your chopping utensil and chop up your soap base (3 to 4 ounces). You should chop it up into cube sizes because it melts in the heat safe container evenly once you pop it into the microwave later.

Step #2: After chopping your soap base into cubes, you can put it all in the heat safe container or your double boiler. It's also best to cover the heat safe container with a plastic wrap so that the soap gets to keep its moisture inside.

Step #3: Next step is to place it in your microwave for about 30 seconds. This is the ideal time that your soap base needs to create a good heat formation without scorching or boiling it. If you happen to boil or scorch it, the soap base will not only smell bad but also turns into a yellowish color. You may still use it but don't expect it to have a great quality.

Step #4: Once the soap base is already thoroughly melted in your double boiler/ microwave, you can now add the blue – mix labcolor. Use your dropper and just take 1 to 2 drops so that your clear base soap will become a clear blue base soap. Stir it up nicely.

Step #5: You can now add essential or fragrance oil (preferably a clear one so that when it's mixed it will not result into a yellowish clear soap base). Take 1 to 2 drops of the fragrance oil and mix it up using a spoon. Spray a bit of rubbing alcohol in it.

Step #6: After doing step #5, you can now pour the soap solution into your soap mold. Once you're done, you can now take your small object and spray it with rubbing alcohol so that the material will have surface adhesion.

Step #7: Place the tiny object you want to embed in your clear soap base and then spray it with rubbing alcohol again. You need to wait for around 5 minutes before doing another layer in the soap base. Make sure to let the first layer harden up before you do the next.

Step #8: Once the first layer is good to go, you can now pour in the second layer. First you need to melt ½ ounce of clear soap base, once it's melted up, you can now mix aqua labcolor (about 1 to 2 drops).

Step #9: You can now put a pinch of the iridescent glitter to make your soap stand out. Keep in mind though that you need to use a skin – safe glitter and not just any kind of glitter you use for scrapbooking. Mix the aqua labcolor and the glitter nice and well.

Step #10: Don't forget to spray a bit of alcohol in the mixture before pouring the second layer into your clear soap base that contains the embedded object. After pouring it, spray a bit of alcohol again to get rid of any surface bubbles. Let it completely harden and voila! You're done!

Embedding Soap Objects in Melt & Pour Soap

Let's Get Started!

Here's the materials you'll need if you want to embed a soap within the soap base:

- 2 pounds of soap base (white)
- ½ ounce of fragrance oil (optional)
- 2 ½ pounds of loaf mold
- Soap embedded objects (preferably made out of non – bleeding soap)
- Spoon
- Dropper
- Heat safe container (large)
- Spray bottle (filled with rubbing alcohol)

Step by Step Procedure:

Step #1: Make sure to melt your (2 pounds) of clear soap base using your heat safe container in the microwave or double boiler for around 30 seconds.

Step #2: Once the white soap base has already melted, you can now use your dropper to add any fragrance you desire.

If the embedded soap objects already contain colorants and fragrance, then you don't need to put another in your white soap base. But if you still want to add fragrance in the white soap base, you can add in ½ ounces of it and mix it up nicely.

Step #3: Pour a layer of the melted white soap base into the loaf mold and spray it with alcohol. Take a couple of the embedded soap objects and spread it over. Spray it with alcohol again. Wait for it to harden a bit.

Step #4: Add another layer of white soap base on top of it, spray alcohol and put another batch of soap embedded objects. Keep repeating the same steps until you've poured in your entire white soap base or until the loaf mold is filled up.

Step #5: The soap base will harden for around 4 hours before you can cut it up into bars.

Chapter Three: Double – Pour, Four – Pour, Morphing and Fading Techniques

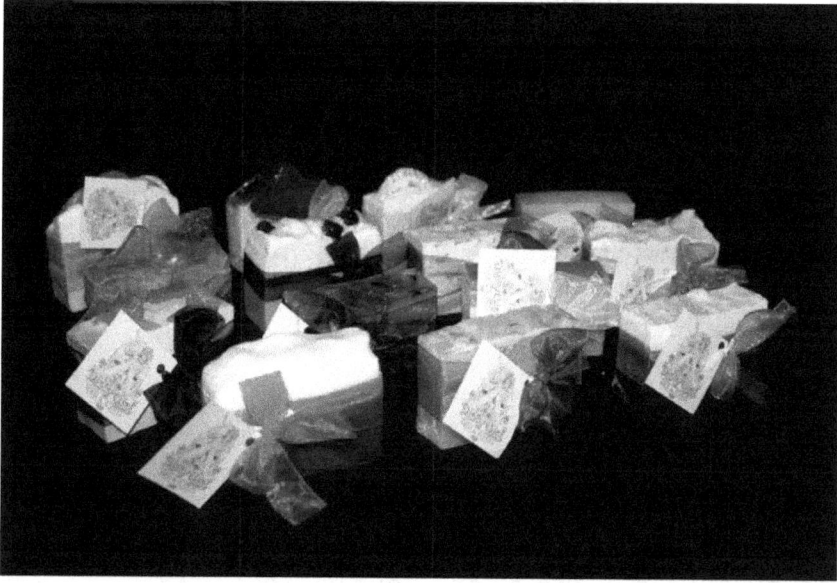

In this chapter, you'll learn the step by step procedure of creating a double – pour and four – pour soap base. These techniques will help you in getting familiar with the process of making advanced melt and pour methods that you'll see in the next chapters. You'll also learn how to do a morphing and fading technique like creating a tie – dye soap with a UV inhibitor and Vanilla – colored stabilizer to ensure that the colorants won't easily fade especially when exposed to direct sunlight, or won't migrate during the layering phase.

The Double Pour

This technique is quite a versatile technique for beginners. The method mostly relies on temperature to create a unique and appealing soap. This section will provide you with tips and steps on how you can properly do a double pour and tie – dye on your soap. You can also let your kids get involved in this process.

Let's Get Started!

Here's the materials you'll need if you want to create a double pour in your melt and pour base soap:

- Soap base (must be clear)
- Gold Mica
- Energy fragrance
- Orange Mica
- Loaf mold
- Soap mold
- Small cups or containers for mixing the fragrances
- Spoon
- Dropper
- Heat safe container (large)

- Spray bottle (filled with rubbing alcohol)

Here are the tips and tricks that you need to know before we proceed on the step by step procedure.

Tip #1: It's best if you use a non – bleeding color just like what we've discussed in the previous chapter. You may choose to use a non – bleeding oxide and micas to avoid the colors from migrating all over your end product.

Tip #2: Temperature is an essential part of the double pour technique. When a melt and pour soap base cools down, it tends to get more viscous as it allows the soap to stay on both sides of the soap mold in a straight line. You wouldn't want a hot soap because it will not result into a perfect shaped mold. Ideally, the temperature of the clear base soap for double pour should be between 130 degrees and 135 degrees in your loaf mold, whereas for a single mold, it should be between 120 and 130 degrees in temperature.

Step by Step Procedure for Double Pour Loaf Mold Soap:

Step #1: Make sure to melt your (2 pounds) of clear soap base using your heat safe container in the microwave or double boiler. Just like the basic steps in previous exercises. You have to create 2 sets of melted clear soap base; one for the fragrance mixture and the colorant mixture.

Step #2: Once the clear soap bases are already melted, you can now use your dropper to add the energy fragrance (or any discoloring fragrance you desire). Discoloring fragrances doesn't contain any vanilla which is why your end product won't go brown in color.

Step #3: Now on your second set of melted soap base, have a few drops of the orange mica and gold mica and mix it up with a spoon.

Step #4: Spray a bit of rubbing alcohol in both mixtures as well. The discoloring fragrance we used in this exercise is non – contrasting colors and they are non – bleeding colorants.

Step #5: After mixing it all up, it's now time to check the temperature of each of the melted soap base. Remember the tip about temperature measurement; use a thermometer or check the viscosity of the soap base – a thicker soap base is ideal.

Step #6: The next step is to do a double pour layer. The most important thing to remember if you will do this technique in a loaf mold is to pour the heat containers (fragrance mix and colorant mix) from opposite ends of the loaf mold. Do it in a slow manner. Your soap bases will go together and meet on the center.

Step #7: After pouring it all in, spray alcohol in it and wait for around 4 hours for it to harden.

Step by Step Procedure for Double Pour Single Mold Soap:

Step #1: Make sure to melt your (2 pounds) of clear soap base using your heat safe container in the microwave or double boiler. Just like the basic steps in previous exercises.

You have to create 2 sets of melted clear soap base; one for the fragrance mixture and the colorant mixture.

Step #2: Once the clear soap bases are already melted, you can now use your dropper to add the energy fragrance (or any discoloring fragrance you desire). Discoloring fragrances doesn't contain any vanilla which is why your end product won't go brown in color.

Step #3: Now on your second set of melted soap base, have a few drops of the orange mica and gold mica and mix it up with a spoon.

Step #4: Spray a bit of rubbing alcohol in both mixtures as well. The discoloring fragrance we used in this exercise is non – contrasting colors and they are non – bleeding colorants.

Step #5: After mixing it all up, it's now time to check the temperature of each of the melted soap base. Remember the tip about temperature measurement; use a thermometer or check the viscosity of the soap base – a thicker soap base is ideal.

Step #6: The next step is to do a double pour layer. The most important thing to remember if you will do this technique in a soap mold is to pour the heat containers (fragrance mix and colorant mix) from opposite ends of the basic shape mold. Do it in a slow manner. Your soap bases will go together and meet on the center.

Step #7: After pouring it all in, spray alcohol in it and wait for around 4 hours for it to harden.

Tie – Dyed Soap and Four Pour Soap

This section will teach you how to pour four different colors into different mold sizes allowing you to create an entirely new bar soap. You can opt to use bleeding colors like labcolor or food coloring that is food, drug and cosmetic approved for your tie – dyed soap. For this exercise, we're going to use non – bleeding colors; you can also ask your children for help on this method later on.

Let's Get Started!

Here's the materials you'll need if you want to create a four - pour in your melt and pour base soap:

- Soap base (must be clear)
- Merlot Mica
- Copper Mica
- Heavy Gold Mica
- Light gold Mica
- Basic shapes mold
- Heat safe containers (4)
- Fragrance oil
- Spoons
- Droppers
- Spray bottle with rubbing alcohol

Step by Step Procedure:

Step #1: Make sure to melt your (2 pounds) of clear soap base using your heat safe container in the microwave or double boiler. Just like the basic steps in previous exercises. You have to create 4 sets of melted clear soap base; one for each fragrances and colorants.

Step #2: Once the clear soap bases have already melted, you can now use your dropper to add the fragrances (or any discoloring fragrance you desire) on your first two sets of melted clear soap base. Discoloring fragrances doesn't contain any vanilla which is why your end product won't go brown in color.

Step #3: Now on your third and fourth set of melted soap base, have a few drops of the heavy gold mica and light gold mica and mix it up with a spoon – it should be mixed up on separate containers.

Step #4: Spray a bit of rubbing alcohol in all of your mixtures.

Step #5: After mixing it all up, it's now time to check the temperature of each of the melted soap base. Remember the tip about temperature measurement; use a thermometer or check the viscosity of the soap base – a thicker soap base is ideal.

Step #6: The next step is to do a four pour layer. The most important thing to remember if you will do this technique in a soap mold is to pour the heat containers from each end of the basic shape mold. Do it in a slow manner. Your soap bases will go together and meet on the center. This is where you need a helping hand from your children since you need to do the four – pour simultaneously.

Step #7: After pouring it all in, spray alcohol in it and wait for around 4 hours for it to harden.

Morphing and Fading Technique for Melt and Pour Soap

In this section, you're going to learn how simple ingredients can help your finished product look just the way you want them. The ingredients we will use in this technique are UV inhibitor and Vanilla – color stabilizer.

UV Inhibitor

The UV inhibitor will help keep the colors of your soap bright even if it is exposed in sunlight. As you know, colors fade when it's exposed to UV light – this is where a UV inhibitor comes in handy. When buying one, make sure that it is skin or body – safe UV inhibitor that's designed for soap – making and not candles.

Various colors will fade if exposed under direct light of the sun such as those on a window display. It includes the following:

- Dye colors such as labcolors and food colors
- Ultramarines particularly blue and violet
- Other pigment colors
- Other food, drug, and cosmetic colors

Vanilla – Color Stabilizer

Aside from the UV inhibitor, you can also use another fragrance additive which is the Vanilla – color stabilizer. It's commonly used in keeping vanillas white. Various fragrance oils contains vanilla but these fragrances will become fade and brown in your finished product which is why you need the aid of the Vanilla – color stabilizer. Make sure to test the fragrance oils you will use with the stabilizer because some might not work out well.

Let's Get Started!

Here's the materials you'll need if you want to create a melt and pour base soap with a UV inhibitor:

- 4 ounces of soap base (must be clear)
- Peach labcolor
- Peach fragrance
- 3 grams of UV inhibitor
- Soap mold
- Small cups or containers for mixing the fragrances
- Spoon
- Dropper
- Heat safe container (large)
- Spray bottle (filled with rubbing alcohol)

Just a reminder though, UV inhibitors help keep the colors on your soap bright even when exposed to sunlight but it's not always a guarantee. To ensure that you are using a quality UV inhibitor, you must test the formulation and colorants you desire with the UV inhibitor before you put them out there.

Step by Step Procedure:

Step #1: Make sure to melt your (1/4 to ¾ pounds) of clear soap base using your heat safe container in the microwave or double boiler. Just like the basic steps in previous exercises.

Step #2: Your UV inhibitor can easily dissolve in your soap when you mix it with the fragrance oil of your desire. For this example, we are only making around 4 oz. of soap, so you just need around 3 grams of UV inhibitor. Use a dropper and put 1 to 2 drops of your fragrance oil into your UV inhibitor mix.

Step #3: Next mix in the colorant into your melted clear base soap before pouring in the fragrance oil and UV inhibitor mixture. Stir it up nicely.

Step #4: After pouring it all in your basic shape mold, spray alcohol in it and wait for around 4 hours for it to harden.

Let's Get Started!

Here's the materials you'll need if you want to create a melt and pour base soap with a Vanilla – color stabilizer:

- 4 ounces of white soap base
- 3 ml. of vanilla – color stabilizer
- 3 ml. of vanilla bean fragrance oil
- Soap mold
- Small cups or containers for mixing the fragrances
- Spoon
- Dropper
- Heat safe container (large)
- Spray bottle (filled with rubbing alcohol)

Step by Step Procedure:

Step #1: Make sure to melt your (1/4 to ¾ pounds) of white soap base using your heat safe container in the microwave or double boiler. Just like the basic steps in previous exercises.

Step #2: The vanilla – color stabilizer must be used in equal proportions of your fragrance oil. Take a few drops of fragrance oil and mix it with the vanilla – color stabilizer.

Step #3: Pour the mix into your melted white soap base. Use a spoon to mix it all up before pouring it into the soap mold. Don't forget to spray it with rubbing alcohol to avoid any ripples on the surface.

Chapter Four: Advanced Melt and Pour Techniques: Clam Shell Soap and Candy Soap

In this chapter, you'll get to learn how to create slightly complicated types of melt and pour base soaps. You'll get to create the popular clam shell soap and candy soap that you and your kids will surely love. This is surely a great practice for you to apply the basic steps you learned from the previous chapters, and it will also give you a pre – requisite on other advance soap making techniques in the upcoming pages.

How to Make Melt and Pour Clam Shell Soaps

In this section, you'll learn a slightly advance melt and pour technique. We're going to start with clam shell soaps! Check out the step by step guide below:

Let's Get Started!

Here's the materials you'll need if you want to create a clam shell soap. The exercise below will enable you to create around 6 to 8 bars of clam shell soaps:

- 2 pounds of soap base (must be clear)
- 6 ounces of soap base (white)
- 1 ounce of sea moss fragrance
- Liquid brown - colored oxide
- Liquid green – chrome oxide
- Liquid black – oxide
- Clam shell soap mold
- Gold Mica
- Small cups or containers for mixing the fragrances/ colorants

- Whisk

- Spoon/ Fork

- Dropper

- 3 Heat safe containers (large)

- Spray bottle (filled with rubbing alcohol)

Step by Step Procedure:

Step #1: The first thing you need to do is to use your chopping utensil and chop up your soap base. You should chop it up into cube sizes because it melts in the heat safe container evenly once you pop it into the microwave later.

Step #2: After chopping your soap base into cubes, you can put it all in the heat safe container or your double boiler. It's also best to cover the heat safe container with a plastic wrap so that the soap gets to keep its moisture inside.

Step #3: Next step is to place it in your microwave for about 30 seconds. This is the ideal time that your soap base needs to create a good heat formation without scorching or boiling it. If you happen to boil or scorch it, the soap base will not only smell bad but also turns into a yellowish color. You may still use it but don't expect it to have a great quality.

Step #4: Once the soap base is already thoroughly melted in your double boiler/ microwave, you can now add a drop or two of the (sea moss) fragrance oil and 4 drops of the liquid brown – colored oxide. Mix it up nicely. The mixture you want to achieve is a clear soap base with just a little bit of light brown color as this will add a glossy and clear appeal to your finished product.

Step #5: The next step is to take a spoonful of the mixture and pour it into your clam shell soap mold; after doing that, you need to rotate your clam shell soap mold so that all the sides of the mold will get coated with the brown mixture. Wait for the thin layer of clear brown soap to harden into the mold (around 5 minutes). After doing this, you now need to do a second layer of colorant which could produce a darker shade of brown as it will ensure that the finish product will have that earth – shade appearance.

Step #6: Get your large heat safe container with a clear melted soap base, and do the following:

- 5 to 6 drops of brown oxide
- 1 to 2 drops of black oxide
- 1 to 2 drops of green oxide

Mix it up nicely using a whisk or spoon.

Step #7: Add 1 ½ tablespoons of your dark brown colored mixture on top of your light brown mixture into the clam shell soap mold. Spray the first layer with alcohol before adding the next layer. Rotate the newly added layer until it coats all the sides of the clam shell soap mold, just like how you did in step #5. Let the second layer harden for around 5 minutes.

Step #8: Once the layer hardens up, the next thing to do to create a more realistic clam shell soap mold is to use a fork or a scraper tool and scratch away the layers of the hardened soap all the way to the bottom of the soap mold. You will have formed around 4 to 6 horizontal lines from top to bottom of the mold.

Step #9: The next step is to melt your 6 ounces of white soap base in the microwave for 30 seconds. Add a few drops of fragrance into the white soap base mix and stir it up nicely.

Step #10: Spray a bit of rubbing alcohol into your clam shell soap mold before adding a tablespoon of the white clear base soap with fragrance oil. Rotate the clam mold again to ensure that the white clear base soap mixture coats all sides of the mold particularly the indentations you made earlier with the fork. Let it harden up for another 5 minutes and spray rubbing alcohol again.

Step #11: Melt another batch of clear base soap into the microwave for 30 seconds; the temperature should be around 120 to 125 degrees; anything above this temperature will melt the indentations and layers you did earlier. Add a few drops of sea moss fragrance and 16 to 20 drops of black oxide to achieve the right shade of black; mix it up nicely.

Step #12: Spray your clam shell mold again to ensure that the layers will adhere once you pour in the 3rd layer. Then, slowly pour your black soap base into the clam mold, and make sure to leave a bit of space on the top so that you can easily scoop it out once it hardens. Needless to say, don't fill it to the brim.

Step #13: Wait for around 4 to 6 hours to make sure that the layers are completely hard before scooping it out of the clam mold.

Step #14: Turn the clam shell mold over, and gently hold the side of the mold to release air lock. Push the clam shell soap using the palm of your hand. It's now ready for use!

How to Make Melt and Pour Candy Soaps

In this section, you'll learn another advance melt and pour technique that your kids will surely enjoy. We're going to create non - toxic candy soaps (it's not edible though!). Check out the step by step guide below:

Let's Get Started!

Here's the materials you'll need if you want to create a candy soap.

- Soap base (must be clear and white)
- Fragrance oil
- Vanilla – color stabilizer
- Round - shaped soap mold
- Red – Blue Mica
- Small cups or containers for mixing the fragrances/ colorants
- Paring knife/ small knife
- Spoon
- Droppers

- Heat safe containers (large)

- Spray bottle (filled with rubbing alcohol)

Step by Step Procedure:

Step #1: The first thing you need to do is to use your chopping utensil and chop up your soap base. You should chop it up into cube sizes because it melts in the heat safe container evenly once you pop it into the microwave later. You will need around 1 ½ oz. of white soap for each bar of soap.

Step #2: After chopping your soap base into cubes, you can put it all in the heat safe container or your double boiler. It's also best to cover the heat safe container with a plastic wrap so that the soap gets to keep its moisture inside.

Step #3: Next step is to place it in your microwave for about 30 seconds. This is the ideal time that your soap base needs to create a good heat formation without scorching or boiling it. If you happen to boil or scorch it, the soap base will not only smell bad but also turns into a yellowish color. You may still use it but don't expect it to have a great quality.

Step #4: Once the soap base is already thoroughly melted in your double boiler/ microwave, you can now add a few drops of fragrance oil and vanilla – colored stabilizer. Pouring it in the white soap base and mix it up nicely.

Step #5: Slowly pour your white soap base mixture into the round - shaped mold, and make sure to leave a bit of space on the top so that you can easily scoop it out once it hardens. Needless to say, don't fill it to the brim. Pour only ¼ inch thick into the mold then spray it with alcohol to prevent bubbles in its surface. Let it harden and never put it inside the fridge.

Step #6: Once the white soap base is hard, you can now pop it out of the round – shaped molds. Get your knife or cutting tool to cut the swirls of the white base soap. The next thing to do is to mark the center of the white soap using the knife. Create a shallow cut first before actually cutting it to achieve perfect curve swirls for your end product. Then, cut the soap following the shallow traces and do so slowly to avoid any mishaps. Cut about 8 pieces of curve swirls for each bar of white soap base.

Step #7: After doing this, you need to take 3 pieces of curve swirls (or more depending on how big your molder is) and place them on your round – shaped soap mold. Make sure that you place each curve swirl just the way you want it before pouring in the melt and pour clear base later.

Step #8: Next step is to melt around 1 to 3 ounces of clear soap base for 30 seconds in the microwave or double boiler. You can add a few drops of fragrance or vanilla – color stabilizer on the melt and pour clear soap.

Step #9: Next step is to slowly pour the clear base soap to the round – shaped mold containing the white curve swirls. You can remove the swirls first and pour a thin layer of the melted clear soap to the mold and spray it with alcohol before placing back your arrangement or you can pour the melted clear soap into the spaces of each curve swirls and spray alcohol to make sure that they adhere down to the bottom.

Step #10: Allow the first layer to harden up for 5 minutes. While you're waiting for it to harden up, you can now start creating your background colored soap base.

Step #11: Melt clear base soap in the microwave for 30 sec. before adding a few drops of fragrance oil, non – bleeding color, and/ or vanilla – color stabilizer. Mix it up nicely, and keep in mind the right temperature (130 degrees or below).

Step #12: Before pouring this second layer, make sure to spray rubbing alcohol into your hardened first layer. You don't need to remove the swirl curves; you can simply pour this colored layer over the mold and the white swirl curves. Let it harden and wait for 3 to 4 hours before scooping the candy soap out of round – shaped mold.

Step #13: You can also choose to wrap your finished product with clear or shimmery cellophane and tie it up nicely with a crafty string to secure it.

Chapter Five: Cold – Process Soap Making Basics: Ingredients, Lye Water and Saponification Process

Now that you've learned a couple of the basic and advanced melt and pour techniques of soap making, it's time to go to the next level! In this chapter, you'll learn the second method of creating soap which is the cold – process technique. As mentioned in the beginning of this book, cold – process is the old – fashioned way of creating soap from scratch. You are in control of the ingredients of the actual soap, and the reason why it's known as "cold - process" is because no additional heat is needed during the process.

If you want to be an expert soap – maker or take your knowledge and craft to the next level, then you'll surely learn a lot from this technique. Soap – makers pride themselves in creating their own soap recipes which means that you too can eventually learn how to create your signature soap.

Basic Ingredients for Cold – Process Soaps

There are various ingredients available in the market that you can use to create your own soap recipe. It usually includes natural ingredients such as vegetable oils (palm, tallow, coconut, lard, olive), and food, drug, and cosmetic approved artificial ingredients. You can eventually add specialized oils such as seed extracts and nut butters to make your finished product pop out.

Cold – process soap making usually produced products that are opaque and have a creamy feel. You can also choose to not use any additives to create a perfect white color.

The ingredients and oils you will use will determine how lather your soap will be. It can range from very – lathery soap, soap that produces long – lasting bubbles to soap that produces short – lived bubbles.

The oils, ingredients, amount of water, and duration of the drying will determine the hardness of your finished product. Keep in mind that cold – process soaps will continue to get harder over time due to the evaporation of additional water from the soap.

Different Types of Oil Ingredients

Coconut Oil

This natural ingredient is solid at room temperature and can melt at around 76 degrees. You can buy some from online shops and craft stores where it usually comes in a microwavable/ boilable safe bag. This ingredient can give your soap a fluffy lather.

Olive Oil

Another ingredient you can use is olive oil. You can easily buy olive oil in your local grocery store and pretty much everywhere. Virgin olive oil is often used in soap – making. Olive oil is a mild and gentle ingredient for the skin; you can use it as 100% ingredient in your cold – process soap.

Palm Oil

This ingredient is a hardening agent for your soap, and it's mostly included in soap recipes. It is solid at room temperature and a secondary lathering ingredient. Keep in mind that whenever you're working with palm oil, you must cook the entire package and shake it thoroughly because it contains multiple fatty acid chains that literally become separated as the palm oil hardens. Each fatty acid is needed on your soap so make sure to shake and mix the entire package so that the fatty acid can get into your soap recipe.

Castor Oil

This ingredient is mostly used in making shampoos. If you include this ingredient on your soap, you can get huge and fluffy bubbles. It's ideal to use only 7% of castor oil in your product because if you go beyond that, it can cause the soap to become soft over time.

Jojoba Oil

This ingredient is a liquid wax that you can use as an ingredient but not more than 8%. Your soap will not only have a long shelf life but also a have that moisturizing quality.

Soap Butters

It's important that you only use no more than 10% of soap butters in your recipe. Some examples of soap butters you can use include but not limited to the following:

- Pistachio Butter
- Shea Butter
- Coco Butter
- Avocado Butter

- Sal Butter

- Lanolin

Essential Oils and Fragrance Oils

There are various essential oils and fragrance oils that are available in the market, online, or from any craft store. Just keep in mind that the fragrance oil you use is both skin safe and soap safe as there are fragrances for candle – making. Essential oils that are commonly available include grapefruit, orange, mocha etc.

Lye (Sodium Hydroxide)

Before you start creating the cold – process technique, you need to be reminded of the safety considerations of lye. Lye is the primary ingredient in the cold – process soap making but it could be hazardous if you don't know how to use it.

Lye is a corrosive substance that is often used in food products, soap – making, bio – diesel process, and in cleaning drains. It is a dangerous substance so make sure to keep it away from young children and pets. Read the labels carefully before using it.

Lye Safety Tips and Considerations

Gear up!

It is highly recommended that you wear safety glasses, rubber gloves, long – sleeve shirts/ pants, and apron (optional). It is a must that you work in an area with proper ventilation because when lye is stirred or heated it will produce fumes and you don't want to inhale all of the toxicity produced by this chemical which is why ventilation is needed.

Handling Lye Spills

- If you happen to accidentally get lye spills in your eyes, be warned that it could cause blindness which is why safety glasses are very important. Rinse your eyes in cold running water for 15 minutes and seek medical attention. Make sure to take out any contact lenses before you do this process.

- Lye water or fresh soap can also be fatal if swallowed. If you happen to swallow some, make sure to drink plenty of tap water and never induced vomiting. Call 911 or the Poison Control Center. **This is the number of Poison Control Center just in case: 1 – 800 – 222 – 1222.**

- If you happen to get lye water in your body or skin, make sure to rinse it under tap water for 15 minutes.

Tips and Tricks in Creating Lye Water

Always add the lye substance first to the water and NOT the other way around otherwise it will create a huge fume like a lye water volcano that can literally smoke up the whole room and spill lye all over your working area and you!

You should also never use aluminum when making cold – process soap because the lye substance will react harshly to the aluminum and can cause poisonous gases. **You should always use stainless steel or heat safe plastic**.

Never use your food containers for this process for obvious reasons. **Make sure to have separate utensils and bowls** for this soap – making process.

Let's Get Started!

The following procedures will cover the basic cold – process soap – making technique. **Make sure to follow the steps below to avoid any mishaps**:

Prepare the following materials:

- Lye substance (you can buy this online, in hardware stores, or in craft stores)
- 2 cups of water in a heat safe container
- Glass bowl
- Spoon

Step by Step Procedure for Lye Water:

Step #1: Fill your tempered glass bowl with lye substance and add it to the 2 cups of water in your heat safe container.

Step #2: Stir it the entire time as you pour in the lye substance into the water. You will notice that the water will start to get cloudy and warm as you continue to mix it thoroughly.

Step #3: If you measure its temperature, you will see how hot it is, so set it aside and let it cool down for a few minutes. Measure it again and ensure that the temperature is between 120 and 145 degrees before you mix the lye water with your oils. You'll also start to notice that as it cools down, the lye water will become clear. Now, you're done in creating lye water.

Saponification

The next step after creating lye water is to mix it with your chosen oil product – this process is called Saponification. By definition, it is the chemical process when lye water is mixed with oil. These substances will then react together thus create a balanced soap bar.

In practice, you need to measure your oils properly before heating them up in the microwave and go through the saponification process by pouring in your lye water to the melted oil. If you added too much lye water into the oil, the pH of your soap will be too high which can make the product itchy on the skin. On the other hand, if you have low levels of lye water, the end product will be greasy, and soft. In order to get the right measure of oil and lye water, we highly recommend that you use lye calculators that are available online. The calculator will do the math for you and will guide you on how much lye you need in your soap recipe. The lye calculator will also help you in computing how big your soap batch will be so that you'll have an idea of the size of the mold for each batch.

Lye calculators can also help you in measuring the superfat content in your soap recipe. Superfat is also known as lye discount. It is the amount of oil that you use in your soap recipe that's more than the amount the lye needs to turn your oils into soap. Since you're still a beginner, it's ideal to set your superfat measurement at 5% or no more than 10%.

Saponification Value (SAP Value)

This refers to how many milligrams of lye and oil you need to turn that into soap. Each type of oil has its own SAP value. Check out the example below:

Soap Oil	Weight	SAP Value
Coconut Oil	8 ounces	0.190
Palm Oil	8 ounces	0.141
Olive Oil	8 ounces	0.134

If you look at the table above, what it simply means is that you can't easily change your oil recipe without changing your entire soap recipe and changing the calculation of the amount of lye water you need to put in.

Let's Get Started!

The following steps are just a continuation of the first few steps mentioned earlier in creating lye water. **Make sure to follow the steps below to avoid any mishaps**:

Prepare the following materials:

- Lye water

- Heat safe containers (for melted oil)

- Loaf mold

- Glass bowl

- Spoon

- Oil ingredients (such as coconut oil, olive oil, palm oil, castor oil, jojoba oil etc.)

- Fragrance oil

- Stick blender

- Lye calculator

Step by Step Procedure for Mixing Oils with Lye Water

Step #4: Now that you've computed how much oil you need for your lye water using the lye calculator. The next step is to do the saponification process. Make sure to put your safety glasses and gloves on before you do this. Follow the same precautionary tips mentioned in previous sections.

Step #5: You can now slowly pour in the lye water into your melted oil. Make sure to stir the oil as you pour in the lye water.

Step #6: You now need to use your stick blender to ensure that the lye water and oils are thoroughly mixed up. You can check if the lye water and oil properly combined by using a spoon; see if it creates thin trailing of soap on its surface as you take a scoop of the mixture.

Step #7: After blending it in, you can now pour in your fragrance oil into your lye and oil mixture. Stir the mixture as you pour the fragrance oil.

Step #8: Once you're done mixing the substances together, you can now pour the mixture into your loaf mold. You can also insulate the soap mold by covering it with a plastic sheet.

Step #9: Wrap the loaf mold with a towel, leave it in your working area and let it harden overnight or after a few days. You need to insulate it properly to avoid producing soda ash into your hardened soap. Soda ash is the white powdery substance that is produced on the surface of your soap. If you see your soap with soda ash, you can still use it but it is better if you remove it because it doesn't make your soap look good. You can use a knife to trim it off the bars of soap.

Step #10: Now it's time for the curing process. Even if your soap already hardened nicely after a few days, it's not ready to use yet. You need to wait for about 4 to 6 weeks before you can actually use it for bathing. You need to give it time so that the pH is mild enough when applied to the skin. What you need to do next is to just take out the hardened soap out of the loaf mold and cut it into bars using your knife or cutting utensil. Place it in a cool room temperature area so that each bar will have a good air flow. Make sure that each bar of soap has enough space in between and separate them from each other.

After about 6 weeks, you can now use your cold – process soap!

Chapter Six: Cold – Process Soap Making: Fragrance Oils and Colorants

As mentioned in the beginning of this book, you have two options when it comes to fragrances. You can either use an essential oil which is made from all – natural ingredients, or fragrance oil which is an artificial ingredient that are available in different 'flavors.' It's also up to you on the kind of colorants you will use for the cold – process soap making. In this chapter, you'll learn how to apply the same knowledge of melt and pour technique using fragrances and colorants but this time we will use these ingredients to create a cold – process soap. Follow the tips and step by step procedure in the next sections.

Using Fragrances in Cold – Process Soaps

Once you've already chosen which fragrances you will use for your soap, the next thing you need is to decide on is the color of your fragrance oil or essential oil. If you use a fragrance oil/ essential oil that have a strong color, it may affect your colorant later on when you're finally starting to create your cold – process soap. Another important thing you need to consider is how much vanilla substance your fragrances contain. It's usually present in fragrance oils since it helps create an artificial scent and it's what makes fragrance oils smell sweet. The more vanillin substance your fragrance oil contains, the more your end product will be brownish in color because that's the tendency of the vanilla substance overtime. Before you use fragrance oils or essential oils, make sure to test it first in a small batch so that you won't waste too much materials and ingredients if ever you got it wrong the first time. Take it slowly, learn the process, and start small.

It's also important to note that some soaps when they undergo the saponification process tends to lose its scent because the fragrance oil dissipates which is why testing it in a small batch first is important so that you can see if the scent of the soap will last even after the saponification process.

Ricing, Seizing, and Acceleration

Acceleration in soap happens when you add a fragrance into the soap mixture (combination of oil and lye water); the soap process speeds up. You can easily notice this because the mixture gets thicker. This is kind of a bummer once you are already in the swirling or layering phase because it'll be hard to maneuver the thick mixture into your desired shape or design. If this happens, you would want to just keep the soap with one color.

Seizing happens when a fragrance/ essential oil accelerated to the next level. It speeds up the process more than the acceleration level that you literally get a rock solid soap from your soap pot and it will be hard for you to put it into your soap mold.

Ricing happens when you add essential/ fragrance oils into the soap mixture and it starts to create a rice – like appearance or into a granule state. What you can do if this happens to your mixture is to use your stick blender to try and mold it into a nice mixture or you can hot – process the soap mixture (which is an advance soap – making method).

Important Reminder

For this exercise, we will use 0.7 to 1 ounce of fragrance oil per pound of soap. Just a quick reminder whenever you're using fragrance and essential oils, some of them can irritate your skin so make sure to do your research as to how much you can put in into your soap mixture per batch of soap. Read the labels carefully or ask an expert.

Let's Get Started!

Prepare the following materials:

- 7.9 ounces of distilled water

- 3.4 ounces of lye or sodium hydroxide

- 8 ounces of coconut oil

- 8 ounces of olive oil

- 8 ounces of palm oil

- Stick blender

- Fragrance Oil or Essential Oil

- Heat safe containers and utensils (stainless steel or plastic – avoid aluminum or wood)

- Glass bowl

- Spoon

- Thermometer

Step by Step Procedure for Mixing Fragrance/ Essential Oils Into Your Cold – Process Soap Mixture

Step #1: Safety first! Make sure to wear your gloves and safety glasses before you start this process. Follow the same precautionary measures mentioned in chapter 4 of this book.

Step #2: Take your 7.9 ounces of distilled water and pour it into your heat container. Take your glass bowl and pour 3.4 ounces of lye powder. Similar to how we created the lye water in previous chapters, make sure to slowly add the lye powder into the water and not the other way around. Stir the water as you pour in the lye powder. Try not to breathe in the lye fumes and ensure proper ventilation. Set the mixture aside and let your lye water cool down for a few minutes.

Step #3: The next step is to melt your oils into liquid form. It's up to you if you want to choose olive oil, palm oil, jojoba oil and the likes. For this exercise, we will use coconut oil, olive oil and palm oil. If the oil you purchase comes in a microwavable bag, you can just heat it up into the microwave. Once it's all in liquid form, we can now pour it into a separate heat container.

Step #4: Mix 8 ounces of coconut oil, palm oil, and olive oil into the heat container. Make sure to take the temperature of the oil, the right measurement should be between 125 degrees and 145 degrees. You can heat it up in the microwave for a couple of minutes to achieve the right temperature. Use a thermometer to get accurate measurements.

Step #5: The next step is the saponification process. It's time to mix the melted oil mixture with the lye water. It's ideal that you take the temperatures of each mixture and ensure that they are around 10 to 15 degrees apart.

Step #6: Slowly pour in the lye water into the oil mixture. Use the stick blender to properly mix the substances together. Make sure that you tip the blender to the side so that you can get the air bubbles out. Make sure to blend the top and side surfaces of the mixture.

Step #7: Once you see thin to medium traces on the surface of the soap using your spoon or if the mixture is sort of like a pudding, you can now add in your fragrance/ essential oil. Stir the mixture as you add a couple of teaspoons of your fragrances.

Step #8: Once you're done mixing the substances together, you can now pour the mixture into your loaf mold. You can also insulate the soap mold by covering it with a plastic sheet.

Step #9: Wrap the loaf mold with a towel, leave it in your working area and let it harden overnight or after a few days. You need to insulate it properly to avoid producing soda ash into your hardened soap. Soda ash is the white powdery substance that is produced on the surface of your soap. If you see your soap with soda ash, you can still use it but it is better if you remove it because it doesn't make your soap look good. You can use a knife to trim it off the bars of soap. Step #10: Now it's time for the curing process. Even if your soap already hardened nicely after a few days, it's not ready to use yet. You need to wait for about 4 to 6 weeks before you can actually use it for bathing. You need to give it time so that the pH is mild enough when applied to the skin. What you need to do next is to just take out the hardened soap out of the loaf mold and cut it into bars using your knife or cutting utensil. Place it in a cool room temperature area so that each bar will have a good air flow. Make sure that each bar of soap has enough space in between and separate them from each other. After about 6 weeks, you can now use your cold – process soap that smells nice!

Using Colorants in Cold – Process Soaps

Some colorants used in melt and pour soap may not be applicable when you're making cold – process soap. This is because those colorants used in melt and pour soap can bleed, fade, morph, become yellowish or turn into other colors. This section will guide you on the most common types of colorants you can use when creating cold – process soaps.

Colorants for Cold – Process Soaps

Micas

These are colorants that came from minerals on the ground. These minerals were cut and polished that's why they become a shimmery substance. It's ideal to use in clear melt and pour soap because it will appear glittery but if used in cold – process soap they can appear as opalescent sheet. Mica colorants can be colored with pigments and food, drug, and cosmetic dyes but some of them tend to migrate or morph into the cold – process soap.

Oxides

These substances are more natural than food, drug, and cosmetic colorants because even if oxides are processed in the lab, they don't use dyes to create their color. The good thing about oxides is that they don't morph compared to mica substances. Oxide colorants are stable in cold – process soap.

Labcolor

These are food, drug, and cosmetic dyes which mean that labcolors need to be diluted first in water due to their concentrated content.

Whenever you're choosing colorants, you need to also consider the color of the base oils that you will use in the cold – process soap. For instance, if you're using olive oil, your base oil will have a greenish or yellowish shade.

Let's Get Started!

Prepare the following materials:

- 7 ounces of coconut oil
- 7 ounces of palm oil
- 7 ounces of olive oil
- 1 ounce of castor oil

- 7.3 ounces of distilled water

- 3.1 ounces of Lye (sodium hydroxide)

- Heat safe containers and utensils (stainless steel or plastic – avoid aluminum or wood)

- Glass bowl

- Spoon

- Thermometer

- Stick blender

- Soap mold

Step by Step Procedure for Mixing Colorants into Your Cold – Process Soap Mixture

Step #1: Safety first! Make sure to wear your gloves and safety glasses before you start this process. Follow the same precautionary measures mentioned in chapter 4 of this book.

Step #2: Take your 7.3 ounces of distilled water and pour it into your heat container. Take your glass bowl and pour 3.1 ounces of lye powder. Similar to how we created the lye water in previous chapters, make sure to slowly add the lye powder into the water and not the other way around. Stir the water as you pour in the lye powder. Try not to breathe in the lye fumes and ensure proper ventilation. Set the mixture aside and let your lye water cool down for a few minutes.

Step #3: The next step is to melt your oils into liquid form. It's up to you if you want to choose olive oil, palm oil, jojoba oil and the likes. For this exercise, we will use coconut oil, olive oil and palm oil. If the oil you purchase comes in a microwavable bag, you can just heat it up into the microwave. Once it's all in liquid form, we can now pour it into a separate heat container.

Step #4: Mix 7 ounces of coconut oil, palm oil, and olive oil as well as 1 ounce of castor oil into the heat container. Make sure to take the temperature of the oil, the right measurement should be between 125 degrees and 145 degrees. You can heat it up in the microwave for a couple of minutes to achieve the right temperature. Use a thermometer to get accurate measurements.

Step #5: The next step is the saponification process. It's time to mix the melted oil mixture with the lye water. It's ideal that you take the temperatures of each mixture and ensure that they are around 10 to 15 degrees apart.

Step #6: Slowly pour in the lye water into the oil mixture. Use the stick blender to properly mix the substances together. Make sure that you tip the blender to the side so that you can get the air bubbles out. Make sure to blend the top and side surfaces of the mixture.

Step #7: Once you see thin to medium traces on the surface of the soap using your spoon or if the mixture is sort of like a pudding

Step #8: You can now add in your mica colorants (around 4 mini scoops). Stir the mixture using the stick blender to mix it all up; once you're done you can now pour it into your soap mold. Repeat this same step using other colorants. It's up to you if you want to mix in fragrance oils as well.

Step #9: Leave it in your working area and let it harden overnight or after a few days. You need to insulate it properly to avoid producing soda ash into your hardened soap. Soda ash is the white powdery substance that is produced on the surface of your soap. If you see your soap with soda ash, you can still use it but it is better if you remove it because it doesn't make your soap look good. You can use a knife to trim it off the bars of soap.

Step #10: After a few days, you can now pop the colored cold – process soap out of your soap mold. Do it slowly with the palm of your hands to push it out.

Step #11: Now it's time for the curing process. Even if your soap already hardened nicely after a few days, it's not ready to use yet. You need to wait for about 4 to 6 weeks before you can actually use it for bathing. You need to give it time so that the pH is mild enough when applied to the skin. Place it in a cool room temperature area so that each bar will have a good air flow. Make sure that each bar of soap has enough space in between and separate them from each other. After about 6 weeks, you can now use your colored

cold – process soap!

Chapter Seven: Packaging and Selling Your Soaps!

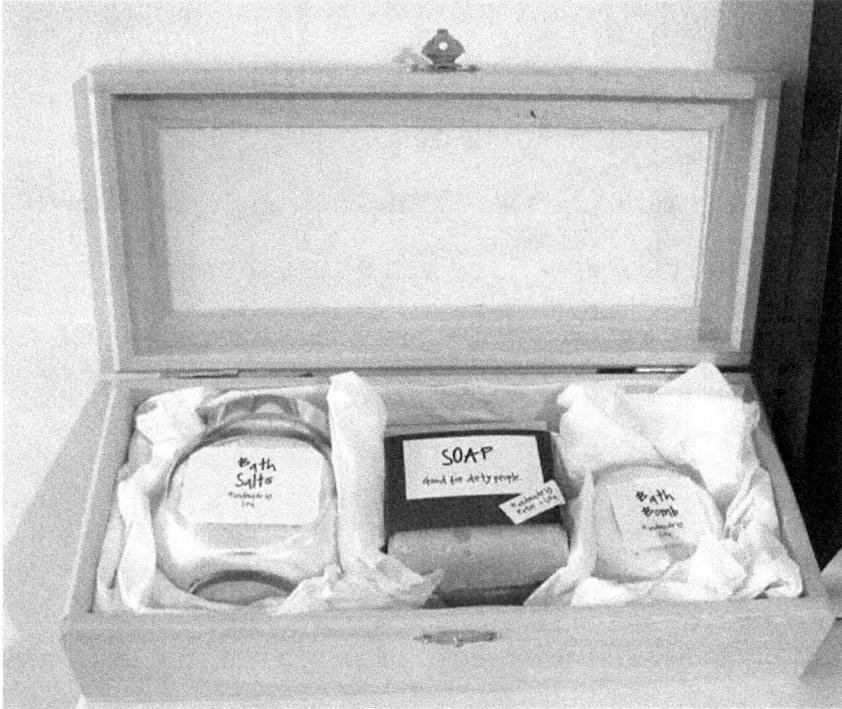

This chapter will focus on several important aspects when it comes to setting up a soap – making business, should you want to take your soap – making skill to the next level. If you decide to make a business out of this craft, you have to keep in mind that you're going to establish a business from the ground up which is why you need to plan about it from the conception of the types of soap you want to create, to packaging and branding as well as selling your products. You're going to learn some tips on how to package and brand your soaps.

Tips and Tricks for Packaging Soap

Melt and pour soap usually have contains high levels of glycerin and water content which is why melt and pour soaps are great skin moisturizers. However, due to high levels of glycerin, the soap can also form glycerin dew and sweat once the soap is made, and it can also appear dry and shriveled if you don't wrap it up – this is why packaging your melt and pour soap is important.

You can use a shrink – wrapping system or you can simply buy a cheap food wrap (clear) from your local grocery store. You also need to prepare a heat gun that you can buy from any hardware store to ensure that your soap is wrapped up in a professional manner and looks appealing. You can also opt to use a rubber stamping embossing gun instead of a heat gun. Don't use hairdryers because it won't be effective for packaging.

Let's Get Started!

Prepare the following materials:

- Finished soap bar
- Clear food wrap/ plastic wrap
- Heat gun/ embossing gun
- Soap box or decorative paper (it's your choice)
- Ribbon
- Scotch tape
- Label

Let's Wrap it Up!

Follow the step by step instructions below for wrapping soaps in plastic sheet:

Step #1: Grab a sheet of your food wrap or clear plastic wrap and place your finished bar of soap in the middle. Pull the ends and wrap the bar of soap just like you're wrapping a gift. Once you're done, make sure to cut off any excess sheet otherwise it would create a bulge.

Step #2: The next step is to use your heat gun or embossing gun. Make sure it's only set on low level. Heat the back of your soap to flatten out the sheet, then heat the sides of the soap, after that proceed to heating up the top of the soap. You should just brush the heat gun over the back, the sides, and the top just to flatten the sheet. And just like that you're done! You can put a label or your logo on the back of the soap.

Step #3: If you need to wrap round soaps or other shapes of soap, just repeat steps 1 and 2. Make sure to trim the excess plastic wrap and only use the heat gun for its short burst of heat otherwise if you hold it long enough, your soap will melt.

Other Ways of Packaging Soap

If you need to use a box to package your soap, you can easily purchase soap boxes online or from any craft store. You just need to assemble or fold the carton to create a soap box. Keep in mind though that even if you're going to pack your soap in a box, it is better that you still wrap them up in a plastic sheet because the soap box is not air tight which means that your melt and pour soap can dry up or sweat. Wrapping your soap ensures that your customers will get the freshest bar of soap that's of great quality. It's up to you if you want to use a ribbon or other decorations like labels/ stickers/ scrapbook materials.

Another way to package your soap is by using soap bags that are available in different shapes, sizes and colors depending on your choice or the purpose of the soap. You can use it for wedding soaps. You can also opt to use wrapping paper if it's more of a souvenir item.

Branding, Marketing, and Selling Your Soaps

Tip #1: When it comes to starting a soap business, one of the first things you need to **consider is what kind of soaps would you want to produce**, the different designs or style you want to create, and perhaps the type of customer you want to sell it to.

Tip #2: If you're a beginner or a newbie when it comes to setting up your own soap making business, and you're just planning to start at the comfort of your home, you can **begin by focusing on one or two types of soap styles.** You don't need to start producing lots of designs at the onset assuming that you're only doing this by yourself. It's best that you start becoming an expert with at least one or two soaps, and then move on from there.

Tip #3: Prepare the supplies and materials you'll need to create your finished product. You need to decide what type of soap material you'll use. As mentioned in the first few chapters of this book, you can do a melt and pour soap, or start from scratch and create your own soap recipe. Consider your safety as well especially whenever you're making cold – process soap.

Tip #4: After choosing your soap recipe, the next step is to **select the appropriate base oils, fragrance oils, essential oils, and colorants.** Review the first few chapters of this book as to the kinds of fragrances, colorants, and best oils are best suited for the type of soap you want to produce. It's also important that you know what kind of fragrance oil and soap additives to use in different soaps. This is entirely up to you and the kind of design you want to make but just make sure it will complement the finished product, the amount you put in is enough, and the product itself (colorant/ fragrance oil etc.) is of good quality otherwise it'll ruin your finished product or the color will easily fade away and make your soap unattractive.

Tip #5: Now that you have an idea on how your soaps will look, the next step is to **master your own soap making style or technique**. This is very important because even if you have all the quality base oils, colorants, fragrance oils, additives, supplies, and even a great marketing/ business plan but if you aren't skilled enough to create basic soaps, your business will never be successful and you won't have repeat customers. At the end of the day, it all boils down to your knowledge and experience, if you keep practicing and keep on improving yourself, you'll eventually find the right style/ technique that will work best for you and your skill level. Never stop learning from your mistakes, and continuously develop this craft so that you can become an expert at it. When you do, customers will surely see that your products are of great quality, and they will always want to buy from you. Mastering your craft will go a long way, and it's also something that you can pass on to your team once you already decided to take it to the next level.

Tip #6: When it comes to branding, you have to determine what makes your soaps or soap making business different and perhaps better from your competitors. The soaps you produce should have a certain effect on people or your target market. This is where you'll insert your own brand once you've mastered the technique in making soaps; **you need to make sure that your soap stands out from the rest so that you can attract customers and keep them!** We cannot emphasize enough how branding is an important aspect in running a soap making business, or any other business for this matter. You aren't the only one producing soaps in your area for sure which is why you need to ensure that your customers will see your company or products' edge over your competitors so that they'll keep coming back. One major tip we can give you is to first observe your competitors and see what works for them. Learn what makes them successful, and perhaps try to implement the same strategies to your own business, this way you'll speed up the process when it comes to developing your brand, marketing your products, and finding your own niche.

Tip #7: Once you know what kind of brand you want your company to be known for, it's time to **think of a memorable company name, and logo**. This is also crucial because it will serve as your customer's "recall." It has to be something that's easy to say, easy to spell, simple yet quite catchy. However, it's also important that your company name and logo follow your branding. It has to be something that when they look at it or read it, your customers will easily recognize what kind of soap business you're running. You have to start with the why especially at the stage of creating a brand. You can make superb soaps but if your company doesn't resonate with your customers, it wouldn't go a long way.

Tip #8: **Start thinking about ways on how to reach your future customers**. It's quite easy to do that at the comfort of your own home, thanks to the internet and e – commerce websites. You can easily post your products online via Amazon, E-Bay, Google, Facebook, and Twitter just to name a few. These online stores will allow you to easily market your products, and you'll also have access to their instant payment or shipping systems. You can also choose to create YouTube video basic tutorials to attract a client base and lead them to your website or social media accounts.

Tip #9: It's also highly recommended that you **design your own website or hire someone to do it for you**. This will allow you to customize your own page, and get direct traffic as well plus in today's world, a business is usually not considered as credible if it doesn't have a website.

Tip #10: In addition to this, you should also set up social media pages so that you can reach lots of potential customers/ big time clients. **Plan your marketing strategy as this is also very important when it comes to getting the word out about your soap – making business.**

Photo Credits

Page 1 Photo by user Ann Althouse via Flickr.com,

https://www.flickr.com/photos/althouse/9822014/

Page 11 Photo by user Amber Strocel via Flickr.com,

https://www.flickr.com/photos/strocel/6497850681/

Page 25 Photo by user Maurits Verbiest via Flickr.com,

https://www.flickr.com/photos/mauritsverbiest/27964860421

Page 38 Photo by user Dirty Girl Suds and Scent's Photostream via Flickr.com,

https://www.flickr.com/photos/dirtygirlsuds/6326564997/

Page 53 Photo by user Corinne Moncelli via Flickr.com,

https://www.flickr.com/photos/hotels-paris-rive-gauche/2564410796/

Page 66 Photo by user Denise Karan via Flickr.com,

https://www.flickr.com/photos/handmadebylilli/15845116616/

Page 81 Photo by user Corinne Moncelli via Flickr.com,

https://www.flickr.com/photos/hotels-paris-rive-gauche/2563495135/

Page 97 Photo by user Lisa via Flickr.com,

https://www.flickr.com/photos/lisabrideau/3150062412/

References

Free Beginner's Guide to Soapmaking: Cold Process - SoapQueen.com

https://www.soapqueen.com/bath-and-body-tutorials/cold-process-soap/free-beginners-guide-to-soapmaking-cold-process/

Basic and Easy Homemade Soap Making Recipes - The Spruce Crafts

https://www.thesprucecrafts.com/basic-soap-making-recipes-517179

Cold Process Making - WillBees.org

http://www.willbees.org/clientuploads/pdf/Cold_Process_Soap_Making.pdf

Soap Making Workshop - OscarFoss.org

http://www.oscarfoss.org/wp-content/uploads/2015/12/Soapmaking-Basics.pdf

Cold Process Soapmaking Intensive - Soaping101.com

http://www.soaping101.com/uploads/1/3/2/5/13255736/cold_process_soapmaking_intensive.pdf

Making Soap Using Beeswax and Honey - Easternapiculture.org

https://www.easternapiculture.org/addons/2013/Simone/Soap1.pdf

Soap Making Basics - SoapRecipes101.com

http://www.soaprecipes101.com/soap-making-basics/

Soap Recipes and Tutorials - ModernSoapMaking.com

https://www.modernsoapmaking.com/soap-recipes-and-tutorials/

Natural Homemade Soap Recipes - SavvyHomemade.com

https://www.savvyhomemade.com/crafts-hobbies/homemade-soap-recipes/

Soap Recipes and Ideas from Lovely Greens Garden Living & Making - LovelyGreens.com

https://lovelygreens.com/category/beauty/soap/

www.ingramcontent.com/pod-product-compliance
Lightning Source LLC
Chambersburg PA
CBHW072235290326
41934CB00008BA/1302